If brass wakes up a bugle, it is not its fault.

—Arthur Rimbaud

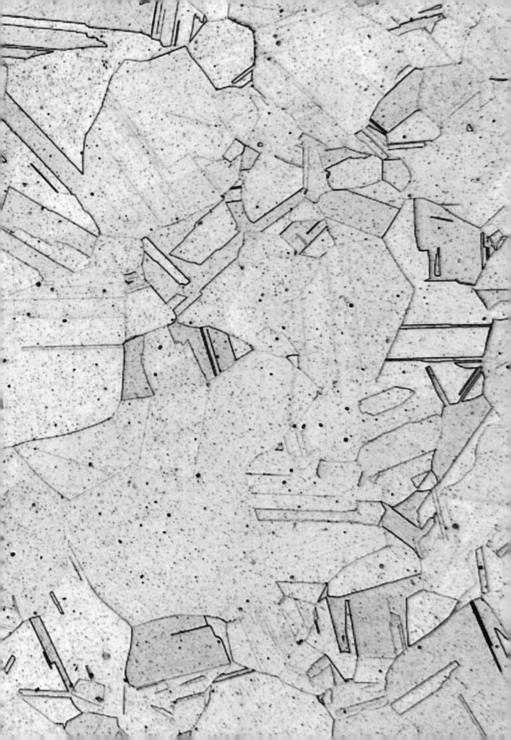

BUGLE

TOD MARSHALL

CANARIUM BOOKS
ANN ARBOR, MARFA, IOWA CITY

SPONSORED BY
THE HELEN ZELL WRITERS' PROGRAM
AT THE UNIVERSITY OF MICHIGAN

BUGLE

Canarium Books
Ann Arbor, Marfa, Iowa City
www.canarium.org

The editors gratefully acknowledge the
Helen Zell Writers' Program at the University of Michigan
for editorial assistance and generous support.

Cover: Brass Metallography Lab Photograph
Jeremy Lewis (samples) and H.L. "Bud" Stauver (microscopy)
Touchstone Research Laboratory

First Edition
Second Printing

Printed in the United States of America

ISBN 13: 978-0-9849471-5-7

CONTENTS

BUGLE

BUCCINATOR

Bullock, buculus. Castrated young bull.
Coiled horn. The long light shakes across the lakes: we buy in bulk.
Give me that oral tradition, that ancient wordy call:
gums, tongues, and mouths mouthing, eat, sucky, talk.
Embouchure—outmoded by the carefree trumpet:
toodle-oo to Gideon, Joshua, and Saul. Infinite
surface, finite volume: it might
be well to mention here that a bugle is sounded,
not blown. O coppery Butte, O superfunded
blunder, zinc-y need. A pit is the earth stripped.
Regimented troops need their toots: Assembly,
Dismiss, Reveille, and Tattoo; Knock Off Bright
Work, Man Overboard, Bayonet, Abandon Ship.
Sayeth the Boogie Woogie, The Boy, sayeth me.

PAST RITZVILLE

on the North side of I-90 near the first

exit, our pickup sputtered, ran out of gas.

It was hot. You asked, "What is our status?

Where can we drink? What do we call a bird?"

I didn't know. We had few friends. Years later,

we remembered the beginning when a prince,

Nigerian and so rich, sent a desperate

email plea for help with big finances.

Back then, we never answered but someone

recently read it to a group of the living,

and we felt the pathos, wanted to give

him everything we'd ever had or known.

PRIMAVERA

Spring is coming, that storm,
prophetic incubator
(a cough, a cough and a sneeze):

Gonna plant some stem cells,
gonna cook some baby teeth with diphen-hydra-meeeeen,
a concoction that can grow lungs or a good buzz like watching
    pennies
plop into a fountain and sink.

Gonna go for a stroll among the calm yet twitchy trees.

Pity this afternoon, dread the television tuned against a white day,
cutting your gums on a sharp spoon,
butter knife gone burnt, coppery blue.

Spring is coming,
wild, frenetic spring,
and the police are here to say clean up this mess,
to generate a document, a policy, an outcome.

YARD WORK

No apples on the Braeburn tree. Some years, they
do that, you say. Your father, the expert gardener,
told you so. I'm gloomy. I see portents, doom,
disaster. Our neighbor mows his lawn every third day.
His name is Gideon, and he claims that someone
named a lamp after him. Click goes the switch.

Start the mower: upside-down helicopter
chopping grass instead of sky. Meanwhile,
the pinwheel across the street, among daisies,
daffodils, and a towering sunflower, spins
like a turbine just before takeoff, passengers
fastening belts, actually listening to advice, learning
how to float on something that's supposed to be a seat.

EXTRACTION

Rhubarb shoots
spiking from the muddy yard
like bloody, broken bones,

like bad teeth. The leaves
grow wide and poisonous.
The sour stalks

burn calories to digest.
Eat only them, and you will starve.

ARTWALK

Water buffalo guts spattered and strung over boulders and scrub trees, splatted in one especially grotesque pile at the rocky bottom of the cliff. Doug, the cart driver (he chose an American name to ease the tourist's anxiety over pronouncing Phuc) was drunk, and the steep zig-zagging mountain trail steeply zigged and zagged, and that's about it: Kate, the American, and her husband, Richard, leapt clear and took these photos hung on First Friday when the galleries offer wine, crackers, cheese, and a plastic tray of fruit. Even in black and white, the intestines glisten like oozy scarves draped over the rounded belly and sloping back, one horn dangling by a few tendons. And there's that one of Doug, his toothless face unmistakably laughing—"We'd asked him for a refund if he wasn't going to be able to take us deep into Virachey National Park," Kate explained and explains again and again over the course of the evening. A water buffalo climbs a mountain, slips on scree at the edge of the path, twists against a yoke, and then takes to air, hurtling 154 feet. I want to know who butchered the body, who chopped up the steaks. I want to ask, "What happened to the meat?"

DATE

We walk downtown for dinner. Thai.
On the sidewalk, a curlicue of ants.
The worm they swarm is still alive.
I'm hungry, you say, and stamp.

HONEY DO

Soon this northern city will be just another aisle,
stacks of ketchup and racks of white blouses

within spitting distance. They invite you in,
say have a nice day, greeters charged to help

find what you're looking for: just milk
and bread. Pay the plastic fee, slide a card,

and get to the list of chores. I'm pouring concrete
into many holes, letting it dry, trying to finish

before the first hard freeze, steel poles sticking
straight up. That pile of boards? Call it a fence.

UNSUSTAINABLE

Four does and a buck haunt the neighborhood
At night this winter, scavenging pears
And apples, rooting compost bins, a clear
Sign of suburban sprawl my Green Friend said
At a benefit dinner for Watershed
Restoration. She's probably right. She cares
Deeply about these things, Warming, and Fair
Trade, local/global stuff. She gave me head,
Later, in her Prius, and when they came,
My moans were muffled. Wiping up, she seemed
Perturbed and started the car. "What's wrong?"
I regretted the question. She must have blamed
Me for something. "You. You're so fucking tame.
You can't even let loose while getting blown."

A RAILING IS A FENCE

A man threatens to jump. A bystander tries
to tackle him (the police cordon not quite
secure). He thrashes loose, climbs on the rail,
crouches and teeters, straightens his legs, waits,
and drops (a long second before the river
crushes his ribcage and he blacks out). Cold
water carries him downstream, smacks boulders
with his body, and finally delivers
him to a snag. His hooded sweatshirt loops
around a branch that bends but holds. On the bridge,
cops can't decide whether or not to charge
the hero: "I just wanted to save him."
Choppers circle. News crews hope for a scoop.
There is none, nothing, not even an image.

SIGN THE COVENANT

Our knives are dull
except one
with a small black handle
that draws blood, hacks
rhubarb in half, shreds
aluminum cans, even saws
wood, but that's not all.
You can carve your name
inside a heart onto a tree.

MY NAME IS JOSH

A librarian with a beard
and a nametag on his shirt

lectures the teenage kid he's caught jacking off
that they have cameras all over the place

and he should pray no one presses charges.
I'm in the next aisle, browsing a big art book.

The kid left a tube of moisturizer
in the stacks. *Action Jackson*,

I mumble and stare at the camera
that dares me to say it again.

EXPLICATION

Exegesis and analysis are cruel cousins,
that brother and sister who would visit from Nebraska
every summer during the hottest month. I was 10,
reverential, and did everything they asked.
He said his bench max was 240, whispered "Hairy Pussy" while
   doing ninja
moves in the basement. She wore tube tops, dark mascara,
and a faded jean jacket with leather fringe
that bounced along with the swoops of her feathered hair.
The next day, in the kitchen, eating breakfast and fidgeting on
   a stool
(bleeding slowly from the ass), I saw in the yard
that the black birds were the blackest birds
and might be blacker still, that they were loud and awful
and bacon sizzling splat on the griddle
made me want to hurt all of them and badly.

ETYMOLOGY IS A LAYERED WORD

Tarn means occipital in the language of lakes
much like ocean floor is the sound a corpse
hears when someone tenderly arranges arms
across the body's chest beneath a highway
underpass and the bones do not move till spring
when melting snow parses the skeleton apart.
Our best words insist teeth clack together
as if chewing tough steak, old beef jerky,
or resilient hope: that jaw fasten, tendon-
snap, recoil of wet strands forever severed
like a beach towel cracked against someone's bare ass
as he or she runs through sandy dunes toward a picket
fence that no longer functions as a fence (only a few
random boards) but still bears the sign, in letters
that were once bold red, "No Lifeguard, Swim
At Your Own Risk." Would you believe that our body
(above) did not mind death, that he asked to have
his tumor-eaten bones dumped in a mountain lake
where once he felt such grace his mind quieted
and all he knew was light and the smallness of his body?
His friends couldn't do it, couldn't take on the duty
of disposal, couldn't foul water with his rotting,
couldn't break the law, and so, he paid two men
he met near the bus station and then bribed
his hospice worker to look the other way.
Ate the pills. They picked him up (late, late at night)
and took the interstate for the Cascades
after getting high and noticed the gaseous smell
a few miles past Moses Lake and said, "Forget it"

and stashed him in late autumn
under an infrequently used overpass.
Now all that we're left with is a riddle of bones,
far away from steep cliffs, clear water, mountain goats
like frozen sentinels, standing instead
above cement stained by intestinal gas and slick liquid decay,
a cavity without an eyeball, just a deep black hole.

BUGLE

100,000 drones above us, a headline said.
Someone must love us, must be eager to know us,
to get the scoop. That's a phrase a now-dead friend
used a lot. "What's the scoop?" he'd say.

                             People will steal
copper pipes, pull wire from walls, feel crippled women's tits,
bake puppies and babies in cars, skull fuck little kids,
drown spouses, and sit down to enjoy a delicious meal.
Lucretius knew, wrote atoms collide or miss and glide away to hit
something else. Slit his own throat. Embouchure,
fancy French for sounding the names of things,
brassy Latin, ding-dong dead tongue—
bucina canere, sing song. Let's just watch a rerun on *Nature*:
"The Funkiest Monkeys." What mother spewed us out?
Vagina slime then tubes, semen from a spout.

BIRTHDAY POEM

My mother turned 60 this week,
deep in that stretch where anything
can happen (her mother died at 57).
I'm 42, and Dante's dark forest, well,
let's just say it continues to thicken,
and I know what you spiritual people
are thinking, muttering koans under
your ginger tea breath: it can happen
anytime, anywhere, to anyone, and
that's why the moon doesn't cling
as it slides across the sky. Fine.
Last fall, hiking near Priest Lake,
I came across a teenage boy covered
with blood, sobbing. He held
a compound bow with pulleys
that looked like they could move the horizon
or at least hurl a razor-edged arrow
a couple hundred feet through the breast
and heart of a skinny doe and out again
and into the shoulder of a five-month fawn that
still quivered. Cedar scales
covered the forest floor, a mossy quilt
to hush the pain, and so we pulled
on the shaft, but it was stuck in bone,
and the fawn mewled, moaned, kicked
thin legs, black hooves like chips of coal.
I told the kid to find a big rock. Quick. He did
and held it toward me, somehow confused, and I
tried to smash the skull but missed once,

shattering the eye socket and breaking the jaw,
before ending the pain and walking away among massive trees
that held the sound in the harsh ridges of bark.
Jesus, Mom, I'd meant to write a Happy Birthday poem.
When I'd gone a hundred yards,
the quiet beneath the looming cedars
was the quiet I felt as a child in your arms.
You were a little bit older than that kid. This
is the best that I can do. Above the ancient grove,
tamaracks lit the hillside in an explosive gold
glowing toward dusk. Close your eyes.
You can see them. Keep them closed.
We'll all blow together and make a wish.

AT THE LAKE

A boy sits on a dock except he's not
a boy, he's a small man seen from afar,
a father, mine, with black hair still, and the doctor
says he's not well, but he won't go now, sure,
he's got at least a while, although Mr. Wood
(next door) noticed red algae on the rocks
and a huge carp washed up dead on the beach.
Dad teaches my son how to hook a worm,
casts the line with a zing. Mr. Wood smiles
and waves, and the dock lurches as skiers cruise
the lake. The bobber lifts, falls, rises with the wake.

YEAH, THAT'S US ON THE SPEEDBOAT

Black bears down from the hills roam the shoreline
for washed-up fish and untended nests to scrounge
meals, or better, a cheese sandwich thrown in
by a bored fat kid sunburned and eager
to head home. The bear prints are hieroglyphs
scraped in watery sand and slowly dried
to fine dust like handfuls of glitter pitched
to air. The kid shits his swimsuit. The dad
wonders if someone's broken into his truck.
The mom believes the kid is sick. She's right.
The bears, a mother with two cubs, eat toads
on the beach and twitch their noses at boats
and skiers woo-hooing a spray, rope tight.
They crash badly, without foresight or luck.

WHY LONG BRUSHES ARE BEST

The guide said

a golden eagle

will wing-smack

a mountain goat

from steep cliffs

and gather

the fractured body

with talons that lift

the carcass—

usually

a kid—

back to the nest.

CRASH, WITH REVISIONS

Late at night, our swerving onto the shoulder
where a slammed door shook me awake. Dad ran
toward a pickup flipped in the ditch, a man
draped out the window, and before my mother
could hold me, I followed red brake lights.
The driver tried to speak, said *pasture*, *passen*,
passenger. We found a leg ending in a sneaker.
My father barfed. The right blinker flashed.
I wanted to crawl through the window and switch
it off. Sirens, troopers, useless ambulance, the start
of vacation. We rented a boat, fished
in silence, waiting for hooks to set, tight
lines, bent rods, smallmouth bass.

WIKI

Sure 'nuff, I'm the leak, the inside Intel,
the narc and the mole. It had to be done.
The drones found it, the hideout, the hole.
Coordinates were getting plugged in,
someone's launch code entered. I wore a wire.
I talked. Asked the right questions. Hacked
data. The text said they'd nixed the strike
and all would be forgiven. I wasn't sure.
Long ago, I walked past a man on my way
to school. It was 1988. He said, "Hey
kid, want some rock?" I shrugged, kept moving.
He never asked again, even though
we stood at the same corner every day, waiting
for the sign to say walk, to say you're free to go.

OK

Do you rename the flowers
after relatives living and dead?
That red one there with an arching stem

must be Kathryn, niece smashed
by a jeep in her driveway (getting a ball
from underneath), older sis at the wheel.

And that one, daisy missing a few petals,
must be Dawn, the crack whore cousin
from Ponca City who said she'd blow you

for 20 bucks. You were 14
in the front seat of a Buick. She took
your money and laughed, told you

to get out and walk home. You did.
The universe is a wildflower. Remember
that blue blossom the color of summer sky?

Dare you to say mama, to say daddy or love
or please. In Oklahoma, the rivers are red
with red dirt and red water. Sunset,

when it finally arrives, is red no matter what
you say or do or dream. No matter anywhere:
learn to rip things tenderly apart.

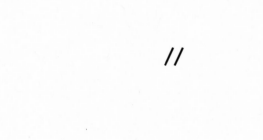

BUGLE

The world is a heap of happy hour
or a copper desert, inch-deep layer
of toxic dust. Either way, these brass buttons
are coins enough to pay Judas, Charon, some Egyptian
toll-taker foraging under our tongues with enough
left to buy a skinny sugar-free vanilla latte
and some energy drinks. Enough to plug the meter.
In the afternoon, a few clouds straggle from the west,
and we walk down the lawn (past a white party hat
left near the path like a funnel into which
you might pour oil, a horn into which you might
siphon dread). We walk to where the river
rivers, and the green light glows, an incandescent tracer
like fireworks or lasers sighting in some late-night
firefight in the Hindu Kush Mountains
or just a traffic signal on main street U. S. of A.
that doesn't flash yellow or red, only says go.

NEVER ONE TO PAINT SPACE, I PAINT AIR

Another jumper broken by the ground
under the River Bridge. Before the fall,
did he consider water, choose to land
on hard rock (intestines spread in bright coils
of purple-red and pink) or just fuck up
and miss the chance-for-survival splash
of the deep back eddy where buoyant washed-up
stuff like plastic bottles and traffic cones mosh
for days? In the late eighties, Robby Brown
told us he'd rather die than rot inside-
out of leukemia. We passed around
a pipe, nodded, nervously laughed. Chemo.
He lived. Kirk said, "Carpe fuckin' diem, I'd jump,"
and sure enough, outed by his mom, he did.

BRING ME THE GOOGLE

At my aunt's funeral, her husband said,
"Marriage is hard." We thought we knew enough
To know what he meant, but the next day, he drove
From Wichita to Buffalo and wed
His dead wife's former best friend, whom Facebook
Had reintroduced when my cancerous aunt
Asked him for a laptop to email and look
Up schoolmates. He created his own account
And that was that. The newlyweds soon moved
And took my aunt's ashes back to New York.
My angry cousin called. His dad's wife spoke
In measured words, "Oh, we went to the Falls
And dumped her over the rail. He said she loved
It there. We kept the brass urn, though, for you all."

FUCK UP

A drowned deer tumbles down the raging river,
smacking rocks, breaking ribs, antlers dredging
and dragging through gravelly shallows—white foam
around the body floating in a back eddy,
finally, broken neck lolling with the steady drift
and pull of current. If only the day
were done. The Scoutmaster fails to see
a strainer downstream, an inflatable raft
bobbing onward, kids touting happy badges.
Look for *why* in the black eye of a Stellar Jay.
Shout the verb for a disastrous decision.
Thunk round rocks against wet fur, bloated skin.
Sometimes we leap into water to *shiver*.
Sometimes we say *death* when what we mean is *home*.

BAD WORDS

Squawfish, Pikeminnow,
Dace: ugly sucker.

Smash it against a rock.
Bash its brains. Throw

it as far as you can
into the bushes.

PEACE TALKS

Guards at the party wear AK-47s awkwardly,
mesh straps draped over their shoulders
like sashes. You never know. The groom is bald,
and his lack of leverage probably stalled
negotiations. Earlier, the cover band Flashback
played The Eagles in a Slavic dialect.
"You can never leave" sounded like "Chevy's thrive
in Beijing." The lead singer's blow-dried
hair feathers scythe-like. He could drive
a Camaro or ride a white horse. The bartender
mixes drinks named after recent martyrs.
Now, Don McLean. People laugh, sing. The bride
and groom dance a money dance. Too much frosting,
the armed men leave plates with half-eaten cake.

ECO-SONNET

Not that I sleep or smile much. Or wish to live in a zoo.
Not that cedars swaying in the wind usually snap.
Not the dog with muddy paws, burdock in its fur.
(Domesticity in the kitchen, quietly
Sliding something out of the top drawer.)
Not the seven horns, the seven cities, the seven hundred channels.
Not that wet fetish in the afternoon.
Not those muddy prints across clean tile.
Not that carving on a tree,
That sculpture of a word. Not alliteration on the letter B.
Definitely not another stuck-in-your-head tune:
(*Gonna find my baby*).
Come on:
Do that in the other room.

LEFTOVERS

Scraps of paper, scribbles on chits, the notes,
letters, memos, and bills, so many past-due bills, the coats
and breeches, slacks and woolen pants, the blouses
and thick leather belts, big bones and little bones, Australopithecus
and snow geese, Stegosaurus, sturgeon, and the Dwarf Man
blowing fire in the gypsy circus, all the stuff stored,
filed, boxed, housed, thermo- and vacuum-sealed, dust-free rooms,
a steady 70 degrees and relative humidity just
right. Don't forget the taxidermy or the drums and horns: trumpets,
tubas and bugles, boom boom brassy toots and waa-waah-womb-
rattling blats to wake and warn, that volcanic
spewing of sound, swirl, siren of storm and carnage,
lightning bolts and the big rush of apocalyptic damage,
a Biblical verse woven into a doily. All this and much more.

BUGLE

Joshua said to all the Neophytes,
"Come here and listen to the words of Tod.
This is how you will know that the Living Tod
is among you and that he will certainly drive out before you the
    Canaanites,
Hittites, Hivites, Perizzites, Girgashites, Amarites, and Jebusites,
the Light Brites, stalactites, East Bound Red Eye Flights,
bedbugs, chiggers, ticks, and mites,
the toddler at day care who bites,
the naked meth freak in your yard last night,
men on bicycles wearing spandex tights, cover bands who play
    'Afternoon Delight,'
people who moon about geese mating for life, dogs whose barks
    exceed their bites,
these three words together: macht, frei, arbeit."
So said Joshua, son of Nun, just before Jericho to the Neophytes.

EXTRACTION

Sparrows ravage the last sunflower,
tearing seeds from sagging stems.

Deer drag wormy apples
from branches, windfall long gone.

An osprey flies three wide loops over the river
with a trout in its talons. I thought the bird

cruel for not rending the fish quickly
at its nest, forgetting the risk of a last flop.

What does it matter? Make it suffer
for being and for being beautiful.

In Wichita, we shot speedballs, and I thought
my heart would skitter onto the floor in Kenny's living room,
a wind-up monkey spattering smacks on a snare drum.
We watched *The Dukes of Hazzard*. Kenny was just out
of prison. Thrasher's dilated eyes showed the General Lee
floating through air. By four in the morning, we were
driving around trying to trade my Walkman and a 20
for another dime. I want to tell someone about the flame
beneath the spoon, how the bubbling drugs made music,
how we all went into the bedroom to shake Kenny's girl
awake, how Waylon Jennings singing made it okay.
"You got good veins," Kenny said, thumping my elbow pit.
I saw them rise to meet the needle, to greet, to say
Yee-haw and *welcome*, smile, have a nice day.

SAY SO

Looking for something to do, Josh lit his baby sister on fire
and texted photos of the flames to friends.
Carl used grown-up scissors to cut Sally's hair.
He told her not to move or he would blind
her cat. She moved. Travis's tantrum: he tore his mother's earring
out and hid in the basement when his dad got home from work.
He was a good hider. Best friends Lewis and Jack.
They thought Vanessa cried too much. They jammed their little
    things
up her butt, called her naughty, got bored. Later, they ate Skittles
and played *Call of Duty* against some old guy in L.A..
He was good, killed them a lot. Lou's mom brought apples
she'd chopped into moons and stars. They yelled for soda pop.
Jack thought the girl's sobs were the noises sexy people made
    sexing, stop
like a mother's no: roll your eyes, then you get your way.

MATT EXPLAINS HOW HE LEARNED TO
KNOCK SOMEONE DEAD WITH HIS MIND

Cup your hands around the folded paper,
stare at the paper, think spin paper spin,
triangle spin. Spin motherfucker spin. It will spin.
You can kill a man like that, just go *pow* with your palm, batter
up. *Boom*. I've seen people fling bowling balls
and cinder blocks with just their brains, and once, when I lived
in Wichita and was slinging shit full time, mostly pills
but other stuff, too; I could get crank and oxy—I love
that buzz—good pussy, smack, skunky Puna bud and kickin' crack,
anything you might want, I knew that
I was close myself, close to being *in that*, able to look at someone
and make them dead, never walk again dead,
just like you can make that paper triangle spin
except I'd think dead, dead, dead. You are dead.

CARNIVORE

To roast, to scorch. To sear, blacken, or char.
To sizzle slowly beneath melting clouds
that drip into white clots of sun. We prepared
the meal with devotion and slow care.
Heat is a run-on sentence about the future.
Chew your meat, leave fat for a yellow jacket feast.

ECO-VILLANELLE

Deforestation protests are the rage.
Their lineage goes all the way back to Zodiac boats
zig-zagging in front of Japanese whaling ships.

In 10 years, bottled water will trigger flash mobs
and sit-ins, demonstrations aimed at loving every
animal in the world. My friend, Eliason, is all about

protesting contaminated silence. He begins
his lectures with stories about mushrooms
deep in cedar forests, how they use time-lapse

photography to show chanterelles quivering
when jets fly 35,000 feet overhead. How a horn blast
can make them shiver. His voice is like a whisper,

someone telling you that someone else loves you
except you can't quite make out the name, only
the consonant "d," and so you obsess whether

it's Debby or Don, but you weren't sure it was at
the beginning of the word: maybe Jodi, Todd,
or Ted. Maybe he just said Do you?
Did you? Don't.

CAGE

Listen with tilted head
for that first burst of photosynthetic groove,
a spitting flow in sick sweet slow
symphonic chords
so close to silence
that this spinning planet
almost becomes
an afternoon in a backyard
where morels mysteriously appear
from cedar chips
spread beneath a porch.

MELTDOWN

O sunflower, feed me your seeds,
let me scavenge your face
as if scraping light from the sun,
give you handfuls of wind
and water and puke blue—
blue sparrows, blue salt,
blue toothpicks, blue ties,
berries, boo-hoo, and sky.

RUTTING

On Copper Flat, elk bones scattered
over fifty yards. Run down by wolves,
torn apart, pecked clean by ravens,
and then bared by sucking bugs.
Not a calf—the rack was three feet across—
old bull hooking a wolf, hurling it
bleeding through air before the rest
of the pack tore in, shredding to pieces.

REFUGEE

We hoarded books to burn for heat, committed
everything digital to memory, and learned instead
the language of clouds: Thin-Grey: dry. Swirl-
Thick: silvery light rain. The pinkish, stippled
threads: Our Veins turned inside out. The swoop
of funnels, that dullard God reaching down
to grab back, stir creation around, tattoo
soil with cryptic lines. We kept a trumpeter swan
with clipped wings. It circled around the pond,
ate rotten grain spread by the shore, and tried
to fly when Mottled Dark dropped rain, hurled hail,
and loosed The Wind. We found feathers beside
a dying bull, bled its black neck into a pail, hacked balls
off, used a horn to mark the drying mud.

NO ACCIDENT

We sit on suitcases by the side of the highway.
Someone's coming to pick us up.

Hungry and cold, we fiddle with latches on luggage.
Darkness (the moon long ago fed to the shredder).

Folding sleeves as if to position them for something,
We unpack and repack our clothes.

MEADOW

Walk slowly. Lie down and wait for a quiet,
black like the inside of a rock, one of those round stones

a glacier left among tiny flowers that you come upon,
just off the trail, and say to yourself, "How did this get here?"

Marvel for a moment as you learn to live in a field
without a fence, gawking at blossoms.

BUGLE

Black beetles know where the most recent bones
bake in the heat, tendons and meat long gone,
bleached white, and if you give them cheap wine—
drizzle a few red drops on a flat stone—
they will lead you to a barren gulch
surrounded by sage and nettles, dirt
burnt to powdery sand and sharp thorns. Hunch
above the skeleton, bow your head, start
reciting verses you learned as a child, there,
under the sun with rocks and brush, bare
locust tree a telling reliquary
of dust to dust, all so brutally hot.
You must pull ribs from that rotting body,
words that matter: love me, love me not.

NOTES AND ACKNOWLEDGMENTS

"Why Long Brushes Are Best" (paraphrase of Brice Marden).

"I was never one to paint space, I paint air" (Fairfield Porter).

Various other ephemera from Tennyson, the 1919 *Manual for Buglers US Navy*, Starland Vocal Band, et cetera.

Thanks to the editors at *Burnside Review*, *The Columbia Poetry Review*, *The Crab Creek Review*, *Interim*, *Poetry Northwest*, *Railtown Almanac*, *RealPoetik*, and *Silk Road*.

Many thanks: Josh and Lynn—your energy and kindness astonishes. Nick and Robyn—gratitude for the edits and deep care with the book. Love you guys. Brian—great friend and equally great "reader." Helen Zell Writers' Program and the Canarium folks in Ann Arbor—blessings for your support.

Henry—learn by going where you have to go. Love you. Lincoln— always / near. Amy—loveliest of all.

Tod Marshall is the author of *The Tangled Line* (Canarium Books, 2009) and *Dare Say* (University of Georgia Press, 2002). He has also published *Range of the Possible: Conversations with Contemporary Poets* (Eastern Washington University Press, 2002) and *Range of Voices: A Collection of Contemporary Poets* (Eastern Washington University Press, 2005). He lives in Spokane, Washington, and teaches at Gonzaga University.